To Amanda and Simon,
So wonderful to be with you for a
sunny weekend in June 2018.
Love to you both.
Hugh and Elizabeth Morgan.

25th June 2018.

Grand
Melbourne
Gardens

Grand Melbourne Gardens

A glimpse inside Melbourne's most enchanting gardens

David Wilkinson and **Kimbal Baker**

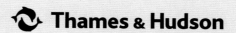

Thames & Hudson

Strength may wield the pond'rous spade,
May turn the clod, and wheel the compost home;
But elegance, chief grace the garden shows,
And most attractive, is the fair result
Of thought, the creature of a polish'd mind.

From *The Task* by William Cowper

FOREWORD

We who live and garden in Melbourne are blessed. Not just by relatively benign climate and availability of plants from all over the globe, but also by a tradition of stunning landscape design from William Guilfoyle (Director of the Royal Botanic Gardens in the late nineteenth century) onwards.

Mediterranean conditions do help. Even with climate change adding a few extra days above 40 degrees Celsius and taking away some of our much needed rainfall, we can and will be able to grow plants from the cool temperate climes to the subtropics – and in a sheltered corner we can pretty much succeed at growing anything with the right mollycoddling! And we should continue to try new plants, new designs and new approaches. As Ian Hamilton Finlay said, a garden is not an object but a process. My 'own' Melbourne Gardens will continue to change, through the necessary replacement of trees and exhausted infrastructure, but also to provide fresh ways to tell the story of how life is sustained and enriched by plants. The stresses of a changing climate will constrain what we can grow, but if we plant wisely and make the right selections, our city botanic garden can draw from a palette not dissimilar to that used by master designer William Guilfoyle (who struggled himself with drought and unreliable supply of irrigation water).

Like all gardens, a botanic garden continues to add new plant species and new sympathetic

garden landscapes. At the Royal Botanic Gardens we have some mighty projects planned. A new glasshouse that will display plants struggling to exist outdoors, as well as demonstrate the very best environmental practice and architectural design in the world – an iconic Melbourne destination, equal to the existing garden landscape. The old Melbourne Observatory will become an 'observational' science and arts precinct, a bustling place to inspire a love of science and nature. At its heart will be the Great Melbourne Telescope, returning to its original home after 75 years, and a brand new herbarium to hold 1.5 million preserved plants dating back to Sir Joseph Banks's collections from Botany Bay in 1770

(and for the first time allowing visitors to experience firsthand this priceless cultural and scientific legacy).

Every garden in this book will have its own aspirations and dreams. If you love plants, gardens and beautiful garden landscapes, then you must visit Melbourne. Even better, live here and create a garden of your own inspired by those gorgeously described and photographed in the pages that follow.

Professor Timothy J. Entwisle
Director and Chief Executive
Royal Botanic Gardens Victoria

CONTENTS

INTRODUCTION

I've always believed that when you enter a garden you can tell a lot about the person who has created it. Every garden has its own atmosphere and soul. This has always fascinated me. I've often wondered what inspires and motivates gardeners to garden, particularly in Melbourne.

As an architect, I have been able to keenly observe how a garden can enhance the aesthetic appeal of a house and conversely, how it can work against it.

Grand Melbourne Gardens illustrates an exceptional but small cross-section of Melbourne's wealth of gardens. We have interviewed over 40 gardeners – of both private and public spaces – to find out why their gardens are unique to them. From the private paradises to historic gardens, there is much to be admired about the diverse range of green spaces in Melbourne.

Gardeners can be owners, designers or custodians. 'Grassroots gardeners', 'green thumbs', 'plantsman' and 'green goddesses' are all descriptors for these people who manage the craft and skill of gardening so well.

This enviable skill will become more and more important as Melbourne's gardens progress into the future. Our population is expanding at a great rate and the green space our forefathers left Melbourne residents needs to increase at a similar rate.

Gardens have always been central to Melbourne's history. Lord Melbourne, the prime minister who was in office when Queen Victoria ascended the throne in 1837, was a keen gardener. His home, Melbourne Hall, in Derbyshire, England is still to this day a much-visited garden and house.

When Victoria declared itself a separate state from New South Wales in 1851, it did so under the Separation Tree – a large red river gum (Eucalyptus camaldulensis) situated by a billabong on the Yarra River. The tree is now located in the Royal Botanic Gardens; however, all that remains in memorial is the stump, as the tree was tragically vandalised along with other historical trees, and died.

The Royal Botanic Gardens is certainly the jewel in Melbourne's gardening crown but as this book demonstrates, there are many other jewels on differing scales. We were inspired to uncover Melbourne's secret gardens and we hope you are inspired and motivated to create one of your own.

David Wilkinson

Right
Como House rests peacefully in this oasis of green, protected from the noise of the city by a fortress of pines.

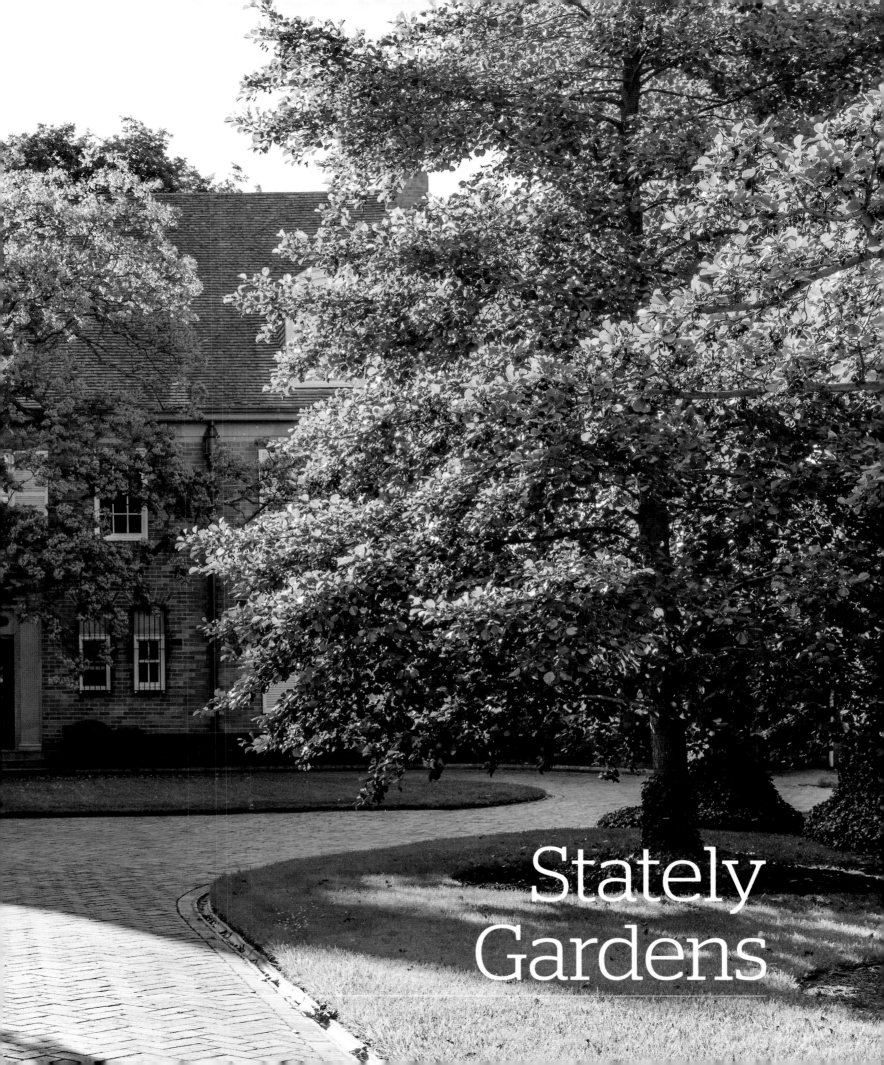

Stately
Gardens

Right
A Bougainvillea 'Scarlett
O'Hara' in bloom on the
property boundary. In the bed
below, *Euphorbia E. wulfenii*
grow in abundance.

BLAIR HOUSE

On the lookout for a larger house to accommodate her growing family, Maggie Nanut fell instantly in love with an obscured view of her future home, Blair House. An avenue of mature alder trees (*Alnus glutinosa*) lined the paved driveway, which was covered in a heavy carpet of fallen blue jacaranda petals. To this day, the view that first stole her heart remains her favourite.

Maggie, who gardens together with David Hall, says: 'My introduction to gardening came at a very early age, watching and "helping" my parents as they tended to their respective gardens. My mother's long and wonderfully well-planned herbaceous border is embedded in my memory. Great branches of heavenly scented flowers filled the house each year at "Lilac Time". My father, on the other hand, was interested in exotic vegetables, a large variety of medicinal herbs, and fruit and nut trees. A well-stocked picking garden was always kept, and looking back it seems there was much time spent lifting, dividing and replanting, especially tender plants unable to cope with the inclement Irish winter. Yet, somehow even after heavy snowfalls, it all looked wonderful to me as a child.

The house itself, built of warm brick, was nestled among several extraordinary old trees and a garden that needed a lot of loving care; although, Maggie reflects 'that the bones were

Blue, crimson, purple and mauve are the colours of choice for Blair House. To achieve that, this agastache 'Sweet Lili' and 'Blue Fortune' have been chosen.

there and they were excellent'. She decided to grow into the garden before making any immediate and large changes. Knowing she wanted to make the garden her own, she allowed herself the time to understand the space.

'Originally, the land formed part of a parkland attached to Toorak House, which was built in 1849 by a Mr James Jackson. Many of the significant trees in the garden date from this period. Toorak House was leased by the State Government as the vice-regal residence for the governors of Victoria for a period of some 22 years. Mr George Lansell purchased the property in 1874 and subdivided it into residential blocks. 'It is our privilege to care for a garden that gives so much pleasure. Over the years our children and grandchildren have played in it to the point of exhaustion, climbing and swinging from its stately old trees. They "help" in the garden, placing double handfuls of earthworms in newly dug planting holes, and screeching with delight at being wheeled around in the barrows atop mounds of clippings and mulch. Life is wonderful here in the garden!'

Left
Stripes in the recently mown lawn enhance the Australian cedar (*Toona australis*), with acanthus flowering at its base. A cypress clipped hedge provides privacy.

Far left
A carpet of bluebells (*Scilla*) decorates the base of an old Oak tree (*Quercus Robur*) in spring.

Above
A profusely flowering Himalayan Dogwood (*Comus capitata*).

Above left
Shrub border of pyramid clipped box, salvia and 'Blue Daisy'.

COONAC

Coonac is a remarkable example of Melbourne's property boom, which happened between the 1870s and World War I. During this time, building on a grand scale was burgeoning and the streets of Melbourne were reputed to be paved in gold.

The house is designed in Grand Victorian Italianate style, beautifully detailed and restored by owners Jane Hansen and Paul Little, who insist that they are just custodians looking after Coonac for the next generation.

The scale of the house is complemented by its vast garden of related vistas focusing on pieces of classical bronze and stone sculptures from ancient Greek and Roman mythology.

Century-old trees, such as bunya pines (*Araucaria bidwillii*) and plane trees (*Platanus* x *hispanica*), frame the historic Victorian mansion set in the appropriate large-scale garden of sweeping green lawns and beautifully presented shrubberies.

Right
A figure of Pan is centred at the front door's arched portico, with bluestone and marble paving on the diagonal in front of the main formal rose garden.

Mixed exotic plantings surround the lawns of Coonac, providing framed views back to the main house.

Giant plane trees (*Platanus* x *hispanicus*) cast dappled light onto the expansive lawns. Shrubberies including pink hydrangeas surround the area providing leaf contrast and botanic interest.

The main driveway is paved in fan-shaped granite 'sets', dappled with light from the tree canopy above.

Above
Cast iron columns support
an elegant arcade that perfectly
frame views of the garden.
Black and white marble tiles
placed on the diagonal pave
the terrace floor.

Right
Cast iron figures from Greek
mythology run between
the box-edged rose beds
with a giant Queensland
Kauri Pine behind.

Right
A Carrara marble urn is shadowed by old established trees looking towards a weeping elm (*Ulmus procera* 'Pendula') on the right.

Opposite page
The sunken garden fountain and pool is aligned with the front door's gable porch.

CRANLANA

In 1920, Sidney and Merlyn Myer acquired a house and large garden called Cranlana, as a home for their growing young family. It has remained in the family ever since.

Sidney's four children all grew up at Cranlana and enjoyed playing – and later partying – in these sylvan surroundings. It is testament to the pride and planning of this Melbourne family that Cranlana remains, to this day, for Sidney's grandchildren and great-grandchildren, a place for family occasions, charity events and the Cranlana Program.

From the grand wrought-iron gates, forged by C. R. Caslake of South Yarra to Desbrowe-

Annear's design, the straight gravel drive leads to the front porch. A formal garden to the north flows into the sunken garden and a fountain pool lay beyond.

Two articles appeared in *Australian Home Beautiful* in April 1934, after Desbrowe-Annear's death, with photographs of the garden and gates. One noted that the garden 'gives promise of being one of the most beautiful formal gardens in this city of gardens'.

This formal style of garden design was in vogue at the time and was championed by distinguished UK architect Sir Edwin Lutyens and gardener Gertrude Jekyll.

With shade-loving perennials
at her feet, this marble statue
surveys the main front lawn
under pin oaks, liquidambars
and sequoia trees.

A formal 1930s sunken garden featuring a fountain lies to the north of Cranlana's front porch

Left
Clipped box ball (*Buxus sempervirens*) in a pot surrounded by pansy-faced violas.

Opposite page
A mixed border of love-lies-bleeding (*Amaranthus caudatus*) and spider flowers (*Cleome hassleriana*) in the foreground with a well shaped tulip tree (*Liriodendron tulipefera*) behind.

Above
Bold leaf contrasts give drama to this long border, including ginger lily, grasses and a large gymea lily in the foreground.

Right
The monochrome colours of the
pool and the bluestone house
give contrast to the autumn
yellows of the robinia tree.

D'ESTAVILLE

This two-storey mansion built mainly of bluestone is rich with history. Owner Bronwyn Cathels says: 'A garden sympathetic to the D'Estaville heritage was our brief, with an orchard and vegetable garden near the kitchen.

'Our research showed that at one stage Edna Walling had designed the garden but there were no traces of her work left. We chose Rick Eckersley as the "contemporary Edna Walling" to design the garden, and in 2006 it was laid out and planted.

'Both Stewart and I love the garden. The kids would say I'm less grumpy if I garden regularly! We have seats both inside the house and outside in the garden to contemplate upon. I have a spotted chair in our north-facing sitting room on which I can sit and plan my back garden. My children have labelled it my "dotty chair". I'm not quite sure whether they are referring to the chair or its occupant!

'This garden has a lovely seasonality. The orchard looks splendid when laden with fruit in winter. Spring brings the fruit tree blossoms, the delightful wisteria walk and new growth on the Boston ivy. Summer vegetable crops are important to me – tomatoes, lettuce, beans, peas, beets and radishes.

'My dear old dad told me that you couldn't grow tomatoes in Melbourne to ripen by Christmas. So I constantly tried to produce an early-ripening tasty tomato to present to him on Christmas Day. I also have an extensive herb collection, as well as asparagus and horseradish.'

The front path entrance of bluestone paving complements the hardwood pergola supporting a glory vine (Vitis coignetiae).

EULINYA

Paula and Lindsay Fox, alongside their garden team, have created a significant and colourful garden situated on a highly visible corner block. Huge oak trees (*Quercus canariensis*) overhang the boundary wall that surrounds the property.

For Paula it's the view from her kitchen window, especially when the clivia walk and wisteria are in full bloom, that holds the most magic. Roses, annuals and a variety of trees keep it colourful. There is also a small area for vegetables, and two espaliered pear trees.

Above
A weeping silver birch, framed by two classic urns, is planted on the lawn opposite the kitchen windows.

Right
A colonnade with pergola has branches of wisteria on the left and banksia rose on the right. Lines of clivia in flower lead to a statue.

Mauve pansies and white snapdragons add impressive colour to this garden border.

Above
The rose arbour and surrounding flowering beds can be easily accessed from the lawn.

Right
Espaliered citrus trees and two pencil pines complement a large bronze fountain with wisteria flowering on the walls behind.

RAHEEN

The gardens at Raheen are immaculately presented. Although it is the private family home of Melbourne's Pratt family and has been for many years, Raheen is used regularly for charitable events both day and night, so the garden needs to be on parade all year round.

'From the imposing gates on Studley Park Road, a wide driveway curved through the shrubberies and trees to the main entrance. Surrounding the house were formal landscaped gardens with lawns, flower beds, gravel walks and a tennis court. There was also a kitchen garden, an orchard, and beyond them a large stretch of natural bushy land that sloped steeply down to the Yarra River,' writes Bev Roberts in *Raheen: A House and its People*.

Professor Miles Lewis relates: 'In 1884 the *Argus* newspaper reports that Raheen's architect, William Salway, called for tenders for erection of a residence and stabling at Studley Park for Edward Latham. Latham had successfully founded Carlton Breweries several years earlier. His only daughter married W. L. Baillieu.

'In 1913 after being a social centre for Melbourne's leading families, the widow Lady Wrixton sold Raheen to the Roman Catholic Church, to be used as official residence of the Archbishop of Melbourne. Again the house and garden were thrust in to the limelight with the first incumbent being the Irish Coadjutor

to Archbishop Carr, Daniel Mannix, whom he succeeded as Archbishop in 1917. Mannix moved into Raheen in 1918 and remained there until 1963. Archbishops James Knox and Frank Little followed on as residents but not really keen gardeners.

In 1981 the Pratt family became the owners of Raheen and have developed the gardens extensively since then.

For over a decade Sadie Jenkyns has been head gardener at Raheen, and she relates: 'The garden management is very much a team effort. Each day of the year, there is always something to be done, especially in a garden of this size. As well as me, there are two other full-time gardeners, Mark Kinsella and Jessica Hemphill.'

Egidio Lunardon has worked at Raheen for more than 50 years and is now part-time. He can remember the days of Archbishop Mannix and has seen many changes. He says: 'I tend to scan the garden each morning, and see if anything jars the eye or doesn't look quite right. Then we fix it or remove it, so that the garden is a pleasure to look at each and every day of the year.

So what is growing in Raheen's garden? 'There are several different garden styles within Raheen's boundaries. Around the mansion and main driveway is a Victorian layout of broad, level lawns and huge old trees with deep flower beds for annuals of seasonal colour.

Orange flowering red hot
pokers adorn the side lawn,
with the Raheen mansion
in the background.

The newer additions to the house overlook a Mediterranean garden of mature olive and citrus trees, bay hedges and grapevines. There is also a lawn tennis court and croquet green.

Raheen's garden is expanding to the north, at present, with an Australian native garden area now constructed. Overlooking Yarra Bend Park and the Yarra River, this new garden includes an amphitheatre surrounded by eucalyptus trees, and a bank filled with flowering plants supported by large granite boulders. It has a very tranquil bush feel about it and is a contrast to the main mansion garden.

The garden has some remarkable trees. When the house was built in the 1880s they planted interesting long-lasting trees, such as bunya pines (*Araucaria bidwillii*) by the font gate, cedars (*Cedrus deodara*) along the main drive and the Atlantic blue cedar (*Cedrus atlantica* 'Glauca') on the main front lawns. These huge trees, planted over 100 years ago, now frame the mansion giving strong structure to the garden.

Sadie says: 'We are planting new trees regularly, including a number of stone or umbrella pines (*Pinus pinea*), tuckeroo (*Cupaniopsis anacardioides*), crepe myrtle (*Lagerstroemia indica*), Irish strawberry tree (*Arbutus unedo*) and some replacement cypresses (*Cupressus torulosa*).'

Above
The result of Melbourne's Mediterranean climate is displayed here, with exotic plantings of banana palms, camellias and the white flowering tree dahlia in front of Raheen's red brick colonnade.

Left
Beyond the two classical pots planted with agaves, the view down to the lower side lawn features a large fountain at its centre.

Opposite page
The driveway roundabout has a central topiary feature. Across the main front lawn is the croquet green and a pavilion shaded by a blue cedar (*Cedrus atlantica* 'Glauca').

Family living areas at
the rear of the mansion
overlook gardens of
native and exotic plants.

Above
New native plantings extend
the Raheen gardens towards
a performance stage and on
to a viewing platform overlooking
the Yarra River.

Left
A long shrub border allows an
extended vista right down the
north boundary of the garden.

GOVERNMENT HOUSE

Government House is open to the public for certain events but it is also the private home of the current governor. The historic gardens, while grand in scale and significance, provide pleasure and solitude to the residents.

'We moved into Government House in the midst of winter', says Her Excellency the Honourable Linda Dessau AM. 'It was not hard to see the beauty of the garden: lush, green, full of history at every turn. But nothing prepared us for the awakening in spring. The garden bursts into colour, and we could meander through its different parts, admiring the expanse of the Western Lawn, the ancient Hoop pines, adbundant roses and a garden that is at once stately, as befits a State House, and yet homely and friendly, for the many families who have lived here'.

Immediate neighbours of Government House, the Royal Botanic Gardens and King's Domain, were designed by William Guilfoyle. Their layout has not changed much over the decades. As with all of Melbourne's Public Parks and Gardens, which have helped her reputation as 'The world's most liveable city', again awarded in 2016, their proximity to the city centre gives Melbourne an atmosphere of sylvan charm.

Elizabeth Chernov, past governor's wife, says: 'Reflecting on my time at Government House, Melbourne, and in particular its majestic garden that has such historic significance for Victoria, it was always uplifting walking through paths encircling the house. Admiring the ever changing aspects of the garden and the presence of a variety of birds, according to the season, was an ongoing highlight that brought great pleasure – for example, the friendly kookaburra which loved to perch on the beautiful curved iron fence surrounding the lawn tennis court and the distinctive call of a koel, a migratory cuckoo, which one year ventured further south from its usual habitat.

'Favourite memories also included the magnificent blue jacaranda carpet of petals fallen on the lawn beside the rose garden and the two enormous bunya pine trees on either side of the steps leading to the neighbouring Royal Botanic Gardens.

'The gardens continue to evolve under the care of a team of gardeners, while at the same time respecting the grandeur and history of its origins.'

Architectural Gardens

GRANDVIEW GROVE

Lewis and Sally Bell are the custodians of the substantial, well-structured gardens of Grandview Grove. The impressive Italianate Victorian villa stands with distinction in the company of equally grand neighbouring houses, not only because of its Hawthorn red brickwork, but also its fine architectural detailing that are both complemented by the garden. The Bells can move from inside the house to the garden across paved terraces, level lawns and arched loggias. The garden can be accessed from all four sides of the building, and visually, the garden can now be appreciated from most rooms. An adjacent property has been acquired to enlarge the garden to the south. Terraces of flowering perennials step down to a level lawn with a hedge-on-stilts of lime trees (*Tilia cordata*) on the property boundary. A cantilevered wrought iron pergola projecting from the house's southern brick wall is covered in glory vine (*Vitis vinifera*).

Right
Gardenias in pots line
the black and white marble path
to the elegant front porch.

48

Left
Deep pink walls and green
louvred timber shutters create
a Mediterranean feel to the
balustrade terrace overlooking
the swimming pool. Glory vines
climb above the awnings to give
shade from the afternoon sun.

Above
Classical balustrading
and urns frame this section
of the garden, which is used
for family entertaining.

Opposite page
Looking towards the street,
this gravel path is densely
planted with scented perennials
and low shrubs.

Left
Pink alstrumeria light
up the perennial border
of the sunken garden.

CLENDON COURT

This garden provides tranquility and calm to a busy family. The west lawn, surrounded by its three-tiered, neatly clipped hedge of box, cypress macrocarpa and pencil pines provides privacy while also complementing the formal French architectural style of the house. Robert Bowden advised and documented Fiona Myer's design concepts.

Fiona says: 'I have always admired properties where the house sits comfortably in proportion with its site, allowing air and space so the house can breathe.

'By setting our house well back on the block, it creates a real sense of arrival. Rows of Manchurian pears were underplanted with box. Somehow this works, as the box gets its new spring foliage just before the pears are in full leaf. They are content in heavy shade, throughout the hot summers.'

Right
Formal box ball topiary complement the formal Francophile stone façade and the slate mansard roof of the house.

Below
The olive-green pool blends well
with the Boston ivy covered walls
and the borrowed landscape
of established trees.

Above
Espaliered pear trees against a brown painted wall offer easy fruit picking, with large flagstones set in loose raked gravel at their base.

Left
A plane tree's canopy provides dappled light. Box balls are carefully arranged behind a low box hedge. The gate behind leads to the espaliered pear tree walk.

A broad gravel path allows access to the property. Standard Manchurian pear trees underplanted with clipped box hedging provide simple formality to the garden design. At night, the garden has a sense of drama and style.

A clipped evergreen ficus hedge provides privacy to the front lawn. Oak-leafed hydrangeas complement the box hedge and a stone fountain sits opposite the house's bow window.

MARNE STREET

This classical house designed by John Coote is framed by a garden where the epitome of formality complements monumental architecture. Garden designer Paul Bangay, who has worked with Coote on several Melbourne building projects, excels in this milieu.

This garden's style was celebrated by garden writer Christine Reid, 'New Formalism or contemporary classic? These are just two ways to define the work of Paul Bangay, arguably Australia's most high-profile landscape designer. For the past 30 years he has fulfilled his clients' aspirations with

his distinctive look of timeless elegance and simplicity that he sensitively adjusts for different climates and different conditions.'

Vigorously growing hedges of gardenias (*Gardenia augusta* 'Magnifica') surround the swimming pool. Paul believes that the plate-glass pool safety fence may encourage flowering, as it acts as a partial glasshouse, providing warmth and giving protection from winter chills.

Clipped English and Japanese box hedges surround the garden beds in which roses flower on trellises as climbers or ramblers. Wisteria is trained as a column and Boston ivy covers the rendered brick walls.

Climbing roses in box-hedged beds adorn the east elevation of the house.

Twin change rooms balance this swimming pool, which is surrounded by gardenias and backed by clipped ficus with Chinese star jasmine covering the walls. Lamb's ears in flower pick up the grey and beige colours, adding to the rose bed's infill plantings.

KENSINGTON ROAD

Situated on an exposed cliff overlooking the Yarra River, this spectacular garden is an unusual sight for Melbourne. Perched above Alexandra Avenue, an iconic contemporary classic house designed by architect Bochsler & Partners is surrounded by an equally cutting-edge garden.

Platoons of pencil pines (*Cupressus sempervirens*) line the hill to the house and surround the property. These assist is balancing out the strong horizontal lines created by the cantilevered terraces, balconies and the pool, which juts out from the house.

The garden was redesigned by Philippa Springall in 2011. Philippa has added plants for foliage contrast and utilises blocks of colour from hardy flowering plants such as *Aloe spinossissima*, *Senecio repens*, *Ceanothus* 'Yankee Point', *Echium candicans*, *Beschorneria yuccoides*, *Leucospermum* 'Carnival Red' and *Lomandra* 'Frosty Top'.

Above
Sculptures are scattered
alongside the driveway, which
is bordered by green and grey
plantings of succulents and
low shrubs.

Above
Echium and aloes flowering
together cling to the steep site.

Right
Bright orange Leucodendron
(bottle brush) and purple echiums
below old pencil pines perch atop
the precipice, which descends to
the road beside the Yarra River.

TIVOLI ROAD

Above
A clump of bamboo completes
this corner with a seating
sculpture situated on bluestone
slabs and river pebbles.

Sheer stylish minimalism is evident in this garden. Grass trees (*Xanthorrhoea australis*) of perfect proportion planted in raked gravel can be seen clearly from the street. From outside it is clear that the resident gardeners have a sophisticated eye for modern design both in house and garden.

Owner Peter Lovell writes: 'The house, designed by Michael Jan, was built in 2003. The garden designer was Fen Brady. A quasi-Japanese garden theme was our inspiration. The design of the house is entirely focused on the garden, with glazed walls at ground level opening up to the north. In this way, the garden acts as an extension of the house in both summer and winter.'

'Our motivation to maintain the garden is largely one of presentation, in the same way as we maintain the living spaces within the house. The overall design of house with garden is very much the driver for its upkeep. The plant that gives us the greatest pleasure is the persimmon, with its luminous lime-green spring foliage, brilliant autumnal colours and sublime orange fruit (providing we can keep the hungry possums at bay).

Grass trees planted in gravel give visual drama to the front garden.

Left
Inside and outside living works well in this home. The north-facing pebble garden has an elevated fish pond, backed by elephant ears, Japanese maples and a persimmon tree.

MELBOURNE CLUB

Melbourne Club's garden is so unique as it is the last city club garden left. The club has withstood the ravages of time since the 1950s, when the garden was once considered as a location for a car park.

Three huge plane trees (*Platanus* x *acerifolia*) dominate the garden today. The oldest, which was planted in 1895, is registered on the National Trust and Heritage Historic Tree list. The two more northerly situated trees were planted later, and one of these has an inosculation. This condition occurs rarely in mature trees, and happens when one limb overhangs another and over time they fuse together. In the club's case, the branches have inosculated to form a complete circle.

In his opera *Xerxes* (or *Serse*) first performed on 28 March 1783 in London, George Frederic Handel composed his 'Ode to a Plane Tree' for King Xerxes to sing in praise for giving shade to his sun-exposed and exhausted troops before meeting the Greeks in battle. *Ombra Mai Fu* or *The Largo* is now performed all over the world. This aria was played at a centenary formal dinner, *al fresco* in the garden, under the oldest tree, in celebration of its planting.

At each place setting at the tables of the event, were seed pods from the tree, so that members and their guests could take them home and propagate a London plane tree for themselves.

Right
Heavily planted clivia in the foreground frames the vast lawn area. The plane trees compete for sun with surrounding skyscrapers.

The bold leaf contrasts of
Irish yew, New Zealand lily
and montanoa all compete for
sunlight in the shady borders
of the grounds.

In 1995, the garden had a master plan designed by Chris Dance who was in close consultation with the club's garden subcommittee. This has ensured that the garden has had successful usage, both in entertaining members on a grand scale as well as the possibility of quiet reflection in a post-lunch sylvan setting, away from the hustle and bustle outside on Collins Street. The Oaks Night cocktail party during the Melbourne Cup race week is an iconic event held annually, outside in the garden, in all weather conditions.

Above
The view along the sunny verandah looks out to the large plane trees, whose canopies cover the al fresco entertaining area.

Right
The Bull Bay magnolia shades this corner of the walled garden, providing a quiet haven. Clumps of fine bamboo, oak-leafed hydrangeas and ferns complete the area.

Right
With the Australian flag flying
from the tower above, the front
garden is bright with white
deciduous magnolias in flower
and a row of pencil pines to
screen neighbours.

CAROLINE HOUSE

Caroline House has a rich and interesting history. The governor's private secretary, Captain William Henry Kaye R.N., built the house for his family in 1857. Since then it has been a private residence, the Santa Sophia School, the headquarters of the War Widows' Guild of Australia, and the home of art dealer Joseph Browne.

In 2004, architect Sean Godsell designed and oversaw significant renovation and restoration of the entire site, including a car garage at the basement level, with a suspended swimming pool above. Rick Eckersley, of Eckersley Stafford Design, landscaped and planted the garden, which is an unusual design for a large Victorian house, as it can be accessed from all four sides. The driveway down to the garages crosses over mondo grass lawns cleverly reinforced by a concrete substructure.

Dan and Patrice O'Brien consider themselves the current custodians of Caroline House. In the past two years they have added *Magnolia grandiflora* trees along the west garden border, as well as a verandah enclosed by Chinese star jasmine (*Trachelospermum jasminoides*), which smells 'divine on warm summer evenings while entertaining outside', says Patrice.

'We really enjoy the change of seasons in our garden', she explains. 'All of the brick boundary walls are covered in Boston ivy, and the groves of Japanese maples change in colour from bright greens in high summer to rich reds and oranges in autumn. We love all the smells too. Particularly the daphne (*Daphne odora* 'Alba'), in late winter along the path from the gate to front door – intoxicating!'

Above
Between the elevated swimming pool and sunken garden, a steep staircase leads down to a carved marble statue by Clive Murray-White called Persephone.

Right
Patrice admires the magnolias on the front path paved in huge slabs of bluestone. A large pittosporum tree in fresh spring foliage forms an evergreen backdrop.

TOPIARY GARDEN

This remarkable topiary garden has been developed by Su Dihn over many years. After the Vietnam war, he experienced a period of forced labour on state farms and became an accomplished and successful gardener, before escaping and migrating to Melbourne. His inspiration and motivation for topiary is impressive, as each piece needs creative planning as well as regular physical work.

Above left
A topiary dinosaur is illuminated in blue lights while a cloud-pruned cypress is in green.

Above
A giraffe's head overlooks clipped meulenbeckia trained onto a chicken-wire frame.

Above
A clipped dinosaur walks parallel
to the street frontage
with shaped golden cypress
on either side.

Left
This 30 year old Japanese privet
is painstakinly pruned.

Romantic
Gardens

Right
Tintern's striking red gate set
within the high rendered brick
wall, opens into a secret garden.

TINTERN

The house, Tintern is of special interest, as it was constructed in 1854 out of prefabricated cast iron panels in Scotland. These were shipped out as ballast in windjammers bound for the goldfields. William Westgarth, member of the Victorian Legislative Council, was the client and the garden was rural in nature, in its early days.

Tintern, the garden, was subdivided in 1902 to its present size, during the ownership of architect Walter Butler. The reduced site still maintains a romantic and a magical atmosphere. Architect Harold Desbrowe-Annear designed and added more garden areas, which include fountains, balustrades, sunken gardens and terraces during the 1920s and 1930s.

Due to its origins, the house is classified by the National Trust, 'The garden at Tintern is also of local significance for its collection of trees and shrubs typical of the inter-war and post-war periods, some of individual botanical interest including tulip trees (*Liriodendron tulipifera* 'Fastigiata'), and lemon-scented gums (*Eucalyptus citriodora*) as well as the burr oak (*Quercus macrocarpa*), and a Judas tree (*Cercis siliquastrum*).

Vanessa Kennedy and Penny Dunn are the present gardeners at Tintern. They work together as a team one day a week, depending on the season's workload.

Penny says: 'My design work has been to do with the planting rather than interfere with the layout. The planting is organised so that flowering happens in summer, bridging the gap between the first and second flushes of roses. It is also aimed to give some structure and contrast to the rather amorphous nature of the rose bushes.'

Inspiration for colour in this garden is drawn from traditional Persian carpets. Rich reds, purple, orange and deep crimons are all featured to achieve this.

Above
The deciduous wisteria provides shade in the heat of summer and allows in winter sun when it has lost its autumnal leaves. The wide verandah is used all year round. Clear glass roofing panels above the windows allows more natural daylight into the dining room, main bedroom and library.

Right
An original watercolour of Tintern Estate by Tibbetts, c.1881.

Far right
This paved pathway is planted with aspidistra, clumping bamboo and mondo grass.

With ivy carpet on either side, these old aigiual cement steps lead up to the ballroom's French doors.

The burr oak tree's canopy provides shade in summer and allows in afternoon sun in winter.

Right
Pale yellow irises cheer up
the borders of this garden.

Opposite page
White flowering foxgloves
catch the morning sun
alongside iceberg roses.

GLENBERVIE ROAD

So private is this garden that it can hardly be identified as a noteworthy one from the street. This is the way the owners like it. Originally designed by Edna Walling in the 1930s, it has been nurtured and loved by the current family as a home base for almost 35 years.

The neighbours' tennis court was annexed to expand the garden area in the 1980s. A swimming pool with bluestone paving reflects the huge red gum (*Eucalyptus camaldulensis*), and stunning vistas have been created to allow views of the secret romantic gardens from all sides of the house.

The slate-grey pool enhances reflections of the magnificent red gum tree, which is the visual focus in the pool area.

A colonnade of concrete water pipes topped with a pergola covered in wisteria vines creates a spatial junction between the old garden and the more recently added tennis court.

Left
A bronze fountain depicting a boy
with a dolphin is surrounded by
yellow and white Dutch irises
and budding pink foxgloves.

Above
Simple evergreen hedging
of box balls and lilly pilly screens
the swimming pool.

AVOCA STREET

Often described as one of the most handsome traditional Melbourne houses, this residence is surrounded by an equally attractive garden.

A large oak and dragon tree balance the two-storey building in the front garden as well as the large silky oak (*Grevillea robusta*) out the back.

A delightful mix of unusual Mediterranean botanic specimens are closely planted in pots as well as in the garden beds. Two fountains with ponds that are full of aquatic plants, and the owners have added to the side and rear gardens, giving added interest and quiet splashing sounds to their garden living areas.

Above
Morning sunshine penetrates through the overhanging oak tree (*Quercus dentata*) and bathes the red brick of this classic architectural gem. Cumquats clipped into rounded balls sit beside the front door.

Right
Potted succulents placed under a large oak tree's canopy are abundant on the terrace of this handsome house, which is covered in Virginia creeper.

Left
A lop-eared pet rabbit along with several guinea pigs have free range in the back garden of this family home.

Above
A gargoyle fountain spurts water in to a shallow pool planted with lilies and other water plants, and a pumpkin vine climbs freely up the cypress hedge.

Left
A large dragon tree was transplanted to this new location in the front garden and has settled in well.

Below
A brick folly with mirrored walls gives the illusion of greater depth. Fountains are situated on either side, and agaves and yuccas on top. Elephant ears, bromeliads and a bird's nest fern add to the interesting leaf contrasts

Right
Two plane trees (*Platanus
x hispanica*) are planted
symmetrically beside this classic
Melbourne house. French doors
feature balled bay trees
in pots on either side. Walling's
trademark sunken lily pond
is framed by large tree ferns.

GRANT AVENUE

T his garden was originally designed by
Edna Walling for Mrs Douglas Carnegie.
Gardener Donna Somerville relates:
'I have had the pleasure and privilege of
working at Grant Avenue for Sarah and Baillieu
Myer for 25 years. My work there once a week
involves the general wellbeing of this beautiful
garden by orchestrating its constant grooming,
fertilising, clipping and snipping, and plants
of seasonal colour. It is one of my favourite
gardens, as it constantly evokes a sense of
tranquility with its age, grace and beauty.
We have all given up chasing off resident
possums, and we welcome each Christmas
the family of tawny frogmouths that roost in
the huge oak trees (*Quercus robur*), proud
to show off their new offspring.'

Above
The crushed white marble
driveway runs under the canopy
of an oak tree to the striking black
front door. Standard balled bay
trees sit either side and jasmine
vines are trained overhead.

Orchards of fruit trees, cut flower gardens and vegetable gardens all provide fresh produce for Rippon Lea. The lawns and the main gardens remain green through a Melbourne summer due to the abundance of water for irrigation.

Above
A gravel path to the swimming
pool and pavilion is bordered by
purple salvia. A classic concrete
balustrade leads to the main
lawn below.

STRUAN STREET

Although not large, this charming courtyard garden is filled with fountains and statues framed with clipped box hedging. The inspiration of Villa d'Este is evident in every vista.

The creator of this wonderful garden, the late Susan Renouf, took a keen interest in gardens all her life. From the Nunnery on the Isle of Whyte to Toison D'Or on Sydney Harbour to this, her last garden in Melbourne.

Each fountain in this garden has a basin lining painted black so that the droplets of water and their reflections shimmer in the Melbourne sunshine, particularly on hot January days. The whole effect creates an al fresco courtyard feel, both in its cooling of temperature and cheerful splashing sound of falling water.

Right
A Carrara marble goddess is surrounded by a halo of evergreen Chinese star jasmine, with low clipped box hedge forming a knot garden between the fountains.

High lattice screens painted black give privacy to the back garden with scented gardenias and jasmine in pots.

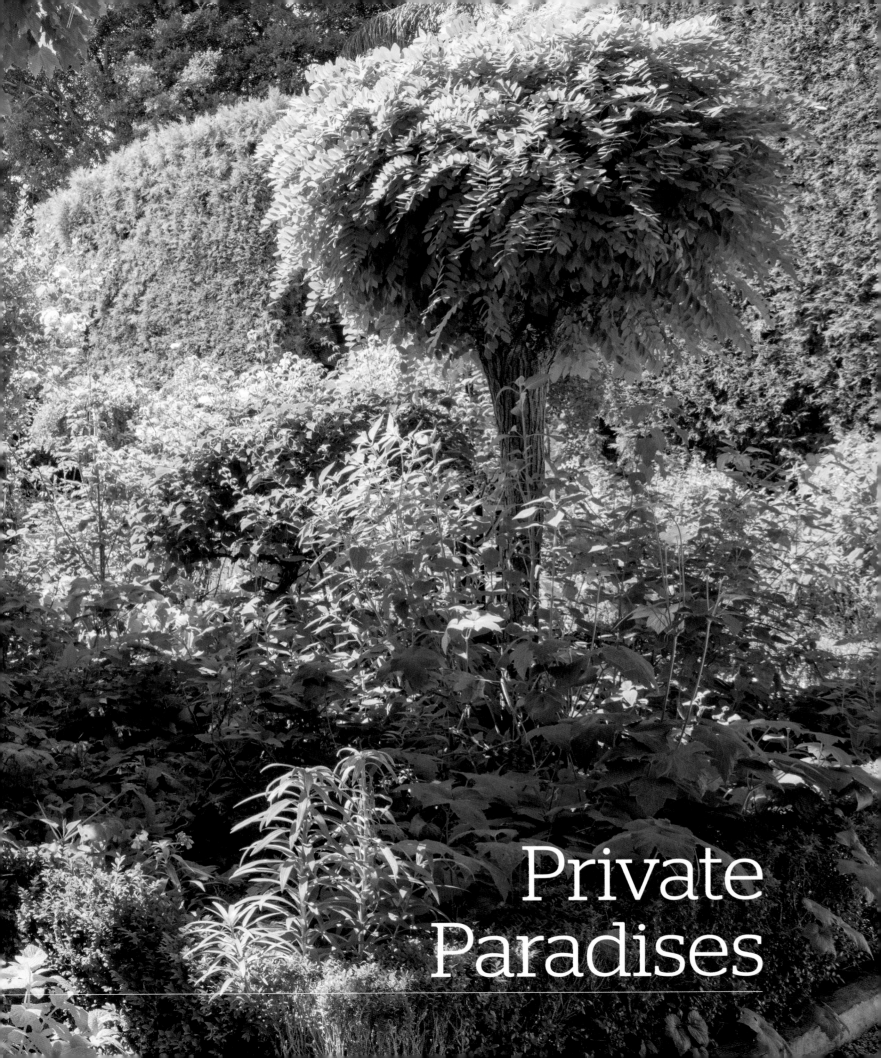

Private
Paradises

DOMAIN ROAD

In 1928, architect Roy Stevenson designed and built an Arts and Crafts house for the Wilkinson family, who had moved from Adelaide to settle in Melbourne's south-east.

Another Wilkinson family, second owners, moved into what had been converted into five flats in 1971, and began to return it to one house with an attached ground-floor flat in 1989.

By demolishing the three extra garages on the Caroline Street frontage the sunken garden was reconstructed as it had been originally. Concrete staircases and carparks were replaced by a kitchen courtyard and utility court surrounded by planting beds.

When the garden had been the chook run and vegetable garden for the Victorian mansion Kalitha, on the corner of Punt and Domain Roads, three elm trees were planted (1895), which have now grown to a massive height: an English elm (*Ulmus procera*), a Dutch elm (*Ulmus x hollandica*) and a Wych elm (*Ulmus glabra*).

As these trees dominate, the Wilkinsons have established a garden that tolerates shade in summer. In winter, filtered north sun shines through the bare branches into the house.

The north lawn flows from the paved terrace to give ease of entertaining in the garden. Summer shade and winter sun allow year-round family garden use under the deciduous elm tree canopy.

A bronze winged boy with a dolphin fountainhead is set in the middle of the pool, which is coloured black to increase reflections. Japanese privet hedges and standard topiary balls mark out the three terraces connected by the stone steps.

Above
Through the decorative wrought
iron balustrade is a view down
to the fountain, with standard
robinias on the right forming
a hedge-on-stilts.

Above
A wall fountain, built to celebrate
a milestone birthday, features two
stone discs and a fish. Red and
white geraniums bloom in pots on
each side. Small tapestry bricks
alongside sandstone bricks were
designed to match the house.

DOUGLAS STREET

Says Jenny Lempriere: 'In 1992 we built this new house with David Wilkinson as architect and garden designer. When our two young daughters needed a level lawn to kick a ball about, the garden worked very well. As their need for outside games lessened, we wanted more garden beds to allow space for flowering plants to enjoy visually from our living rooms, and to cut for the house – both annuals and perennials.

Four beds were cut into the lawn on the centreline of the main hall of the house, symmetrically. As you enter our front door you can see right down the length of the house across the garden to a trompe-l'oeil cleverly reflected in a mirror. This gives an illusion of even greater depth to the garden.'

A trompe-l'oeil effect giving
extra depth to the garden from
the house is created by a mirror
on the fence between two
columns and a timber garden
bench surrounded by heavily
scented evergreen jasmine.

127

Above
A plunge pool and ficus-covered
fountain give the courtyard
a focus under the wisteria-
covered pergola. A pale-green
hosta in a pot on the table
enjoying summer shade.

Above
Sunny garden beds filled with
flowers, herbs and vegetables
edged by box hedges are used
all year round.

129

YAR-ORRONG ROAD

Wisteria vines climb by twining themselves around a support. Some species, such as *Wisteria floribunda*, twine in a clockwise direction while others, such as *Wisteria sinensis*, twine in an anti-clockwise direction. The flower heads can vary in length and can have anywhere from 20 to 170 individual flowers depending on species and cultivar. The Morgans' wisteria is an example of how well this vigorous vine grows in Melbourne. *Wisteria floribunda* 'Lawrence', has long densely packed blue–mauve racemes and a glorious sweet scent. It commands this garden when in flower as it climbs up the north-facing colonnade set off against the pristine white elevation of the classic Georgian house.

Libby Morgan remembers transplanting a rooted layering from her mother-in-law's garden nearby, and it has thrived here. 'We bought our house in 1969. The house was built in 1955 by the Yunken Freeman Architects. We engaged Ellis Stones, when he was working with Edna Walling in Hugh's parents' gardens nearby, to resolve how our ideas of level lawn changes and walls could best be implemented. Looking back over nearly 50 years, the garden has given our family great pleasure.'

Above
A clipped cushion of teucrium and euphorbia on the left with yellow clivia on the right and cloud-pruned topiary behind.

Right
A spectacular spring show of wisteria is trained up the Corinthian column of the neo-Georgian classic house.

A slate-edged asymmetrical swimming pool blends in with the grey colouration of the bluestone paving and rock-edged beds.

KOOYONG ROAD

The dramatic impact of this garden is heightened by the planting design surrounding the terrace.

Garden designer Robert Boyle says: 'In 2010 a complete refurbishment of this garden took place, after our original layout of 1980s had been let go.

'My new design simplified the garden, providing a large, level lawn and walls of Castlemaine stone, sweeping driveways and new lattice screens with wisteria-covered pergolas.

'The garden now has a classic appearance, with a Mediterranean-style swimming pool, tennis court and large elevated terraces bathed in northern sunshine, essential for Melbourne winter cheer.'

Above
Clipped evergreen ficus covers the walls down to the pool level.

Right
Creeping ficus is trained high up slender columns to frame the north terrace of the house. Glass balustrading allows clear views from the house down to the garden.

Left
The green lattice screen and pencil pines provide privacy and shelter.

Below
Beautiful bonsai specimens are carefully nurtured by Betty in shallow pots on her small balcony. She shapes them skilfully into artistic Oriental shapes.

Right
A sasanqua camellia hedge flowering in winter is underplanted with white impatiens along the balcony.

CAMELLIA BALCONY

Betty Spangaro's balcony faces south on the fourth floor of her Camberwell Road apartment. As a keen gardener in this restricted space she has been inspired and motivated to create a garden that she says gets her started early each morning.

Everything has to be grown in quite small pots, which vary in size depending on the plants. Bonsai specimens and vireya rhododendrons suit these difficult growing situations, as they both seem to grow well without too much sun and very little soil. In fact, Betty's vireyas revel in growing in old tree-fern stumps, almost epiphytically.

With a camellia hedge for privacy underplanted with white impatiens for cheer, sitting on this balcony is enhanced by what is growing around you. Betty says her life is made more complete because of her garden, despite its size, and she opens the doors each morning to enjoy her exercise routine on her balcony garden.

VERMONT SOUTH GARDEN

Ellis Stones built a stone sitting wall 34 years ago for the Jeffersons' first garden. This impressive garden has developed over recent years around their John Coote designed house. Today, it is Penny Dunn who gardens with Pamela Jefferson.

As part of the Open Gardens scheme in 2015, the garden was described thus: 'A high front wall encloses an established formal garden, with a more relaxed mood at the rear. Wide steps lead past citrus in tubs around a pool to sweeping lawns, flanked by trees, shrubs and generous groupings of summer flowering perennials, roses and poppies.'

'The herbaceous border is at its peak in late summer', says Pamela. 'This year we are transforming the colour range to hot pink and scarlet moving through to purple and plum.

Perennials such as dahlia varieties, *Verbena bonariensis*, *V. venosa*, veronicas, *Mondarda* 'Donnervolke', *Lepechina hastata*, asters and *Origanum* 'Hopleys' provide these rich colours. Textured interest is provided by foliage plants such as *Melianthus major*, *Miscanthus* 'Zebrinus', canna lilies and *Inula magnifica*. Long after the perennials' flowering period has ended, the foliage plants take on the hues of autumn, and their bold structures provide interest in the garden throughout winter.

Every window from our home has a special view. I love order. Is it achievable? Sometimes – in between chaos!'

Right
An array of bulbs and perennials in the front formal garden provide the rich view from the study.

Sloping lawns meet large beds of shrubs, with a white crepe myrtle tree on the left and buddleia on the right.

Left
From deep shade, the garden opens out to sunny lawns and densely planted borders.

Above
Last season's wisteria seed pods dangle down through the open timber awning. Terracotta tiles change to checkerboard timber decking leading down to the family outdoor dining area.

145

SPRING STREET

Primrose Potter has always gardened. Her rooftop garden, at Sydney's Del Rio in Elizabeth Bay, won the *Sydney Morning Herald* small garden award in 1970. Now, based in Melbourne, Lady Primrose maintains two incredible rooftop gardens at her inner city apartment complex. Contending with limited space and along with wild weather conditions, it's no small feat to have achieved such an impressive garden. Her garden shows an expert knowledge of plants and the conditions in which they will grow given these trying elements.

'Abelias, azaleas and buddleias all do well up here, as they tolerate wind, and then I fill pots with annuals for seasonal colour. Gardening exists in every generation of my family. From the six generation beginning with the Coke of Leicester down'.

Above left
Flowering scarlet azaleas and evergreen gardenias are sheltered by plate glass on the west side of the garden.

Above
Established potted pencil pines mirror the vertical lines of the surrounding city buildings on the east side of the roof garden.

Right
A pink azalea brightens up a corner of the roof garden with a gardenia bush behind.

Left

An impressive Melbourne skyline is seen here with the magnificent spires of St Patrick's Cathedral as the roof garden's backdrop. Lavender and red potted geraniums are sheltered from high winds by the solid balustrade.

Above

Plants in pots of all shapes and sizes give colour and movement throughout the year. Annuals are planted for Christmas cheer. Azaleas and camellias flower intermittently.

Right
A carefully planned 'disarray' of exotic plantings gives this garden a special magic. A soft-pink tree begonia is planted in the ground and a big tree fern in a pot.

NORTHCOTE COURTYARD

Bill Henson moves established trees around like chess pieces in his secret garden sanctuary located in Northcote, in Melbourne's north. As you enter this private world, it gives the feeling that a Kyoto-trained gardener has been at work.

What was once an industrial site has been transformed into a world of botanical wonder. Bill has left the original brick boundary walls, arranged large rocks to retain soil, and moved in established trees and shrubs, arranging them with a true artistic eye.

'It was a car park until 2006', says Bill. 'No trees, no grass, but most importantly, no weeds! Hopefully the poisons were all scraped away before I put the trees in. I haven't noticed any untoward asymmetry unfolding.

'As Werner Hertzog might say, "I am missing the chungle." I feel the disappearance of Melbourne's gardens. And, more particularly, large and old trees acutely. On this little patch of land the neighbourhood was expecting a block of apartments to be built.

I have everything and anything growing in my garden,' exclaims Bill. Although he's happy to admit that it's more of a green garden rather than a flower garden. Bill, unlike many other gardeners, happily takes in the wildlife refugee population. 'All the little "people" have moved in, and their ranks continue to swell'. This leafy oasis is a magnet for birds, bees, cats, bats and possums. 'Whether the plant life can keep up with it remains to be seen', exclaims Bill.

There's a seeming shift in gardening trends that is leaning towards more native planting choices. 'It's funny that we are so obsessed with multiculturalism,' he laments, 'and yet the same people here in Melbourne want to remove all "exotics" in an attempt to wind the clock back. Fascist revisionism I call it.

'I've been reminding myself that once I thought there was nothing sexier than a beautiful old pot with some dead weeds in it. We'll have to wait and see. My lovely mother, in whose beautiful garden I grew up, might have had something to say about that!'

A stunning view from Bill's studio looks across raked gravel to a strategically placed water bowl. The bowl is centered in order to visually deepen the perspective, as well as provide water for birds. Rescued and recycled trees, old urns and large rocks help create this green oasis.

Historic
Gardens

RICHMOND HOUSE

Richmond House is a heritage listed house located in South Yarra. It has recently had a garden makeover, which complements the landmark building on the crest of the Avoca Street hill.

Georgian residential architecture is paired successfully with a classically landscaped garden. Thick slabs of slate have been repurposed to help form the new crushed gravel driveway.

On the northern boundary is a well-established lime tree (*Tilia cordata*), which radiates its exotic scent throughout the garden in spring. Along the gravel drive, grey textured foliage contrasts with echiums, rosemary, grasses and strategically placed clipped box balls.

Incumbent chatelaine Antoinette Nido and her mother influence the overall garden style and grow fresh vegetables and herbs for cooking family meals.

Miles Baldwin, a Sydney-based garden designer, laid out the refurbished garden. Antoinette had admired his design at Government House in Sydney, where he had completed the planting of the East Terrace border. She loved his plant combinations and felt that given the similarities in the Georgian architecture, a similar planting scheme would work at Richmond House.

Right
The street frontage of this handsome historic house faces west, and the echiums, grasses, rosemary and lavenders thrive in the hot afternoon sun. Their grey–green hues enhance the colours of both the house behind and the gravel in front.

Framed by the pendulous leaves of an old Linden tree, the gravel driveway's edges are beautifully planted. The original slabs of slate have been relaid so that the driveway and pedestrian path match, with loose raked gravel in between.

Contrasting leaf foliage provide botanic interest to this bed of agapanthus, rosemary, euphorbia and box. Two tall 'Capital' fastigiate pear trees are planted either side of the front gate.

BISHOPSCOURT

fter a proposal of subdivision was defeated in 1999, the large garden at Bishopscourt was thrown a lifeline by the Australian Garden History Society. The call went out, a band of garden volunteers responded with enthusiasm, and working bees started under Australia's Open Garden Scheme. These working bee's are still held each month, with an average roll-up of '20 people with a wonderful camaraderie' developing within the group attending, Elizabeth Rushen says in her book *Bishopscourt Melbourne*.

She goes on to say: 'The large Port Jackson fig (*Ficus rubiginosa*) located at the south-west corner of the private formal garden, was listed on the Victorian Register and in 2002 the National Trust also classified it as a significant tree.'

The archbishop of Melbourne and his family enjoy the fruits of a productive orchard and vegetable garden with hives of very active bees.

Large lawns framed by herbaceous borders provide level outdoor entertaining areas for functions. Winding gravel paths through old established shrubberies allow for meandering.

Left
The established canopy of gum and elm trees provide dappled light on the gravel driveway.

Above
The mansion's beautiful original bluestone is seen here from across the lawn. A single classic urn is situated in the old rose bed.

Opposite page
A relaxed, colourful herbaceous border of hollyhocks, roses and salvias. A vegetable garden, bee hives and an orchard all thrive in this inner-city location.

161

OLD COLONISTS' GARDENS

In 1870, actor George Selth Coppin took it upon himself to establish a group of Victorian villas to provide acceptable communal living for impoverished aging performers.

He built the 'Founder's Cottage' in local bluestone with white tuckpointing, and since then have been added red brick, rendered brick and feature brick living units for elderly citizens.

Each dwelling has a small garden adjacent to it. The residents can plant and maintain their own plot or a gardener can assist. These small close-by areas offer wellbeing and satisfaction to those who choose to garden in them in their advancing years.

Below
A crop of yellow grapefruit in plentiful numbers ripens on the large old citrus tree in one of these small historic gardens.

Each of these charming Victorian
cottages has its own area of
garden to enjoy. This leads to
a varied mix of styles and plant
material, and the overall result is
one of small garden charm
at its best.

ROYAL BOTANIC GARDENS

Baron Ferdinand von Mueller began Melbourne's Royal Botanic Gardens, but it was William Guilfoyle who left a legacy for everyone to enjoy. Melbourne's Royal Botanic Gardens are considered the best in Australia – the jewel in Melbourne's garden crown.

The gardens have exotic and indigenous living collections as well as the National Herbarium, holding an enviable collection of dried plant specimens and seeds.

Guilfoyle's volcano, on the east boundary of the gardens – has surrounding 'lava flow' shaped shrubberies and extensive succulent and cactus plantings. The original bluestone basin of water now heads up an irrigation system that circulates rainwater from the Birdwood Avenue catchment into Nymphaea Lake. It then travels down the refurbished Fern Gully creek, to the main lake. Along the way, the water is filtered beneath the canna beds, and is pumped back up the steep hill to the volcano. Hydraulic engineering is responsible for this remarkable water-saving system and should safeguard the need to irrigate in the many hot summers to come.

The Royal Botanic Gardens contain many exotic and indigenous plants. The Grey Garden, dropping down steeply from the Temple of the Winds to Alexandra Avenue's Tan is a particular favourite of visitors. Another is the Chinese Collection, which surrounds a winding path between the Tan and the lake, running parallel to the Yarra River.

Terry Smyth has gardened here for 28 years, and relates why she has remained the primary gardener at the Chinese gardens for so long, when she thought she would take the job for one year: 'I love working within the Southern China Collection in all seasons. There is never ending beauty and I am motivated to improve the collection. My passion for Chinese plants has grown whenever I spend time in the beautiful forests of Yunnan and Sichuan and other parts of China. The flora is enormous and fascinating, so there are always new plants to discover. It has been fantastic to have a long-term connection with staff from other Chinese botanic gardens, particularly the Kunming Botanical Gardens in Yunnan. Whether pruning, tidying over the enormous leaves of giant elephant ear (*Colocasia gigantea*), planting new gems, updating plant records, or speaking to student or volunteer guide groups, it feels worthwhile.

'I enjoy walking along the Serpentine Path in early spring, noting the swelling deep pink buds of *Cercis glabra* that flower simultaneously with the rosy show of *Paeonia suffruticosa*, adjacent to it.'

The Grey Garden drops steeply from the Temple of the Winds to the Tan, which runs around the perimeter of the gardens. It is well stocked with fascinating material from exotic to native species.

'The symbolism and stories behind Chinese plant names are delightful. For example the *Lycoris aurea* flowering bulb's Chinese name is translated as 'suddenly the soil smiles', and plum blossoms, known as "Mei Hua", for example *Prunus mume*, represent resilience, purity and other virtues.

Below
Nymphaea Lake is planted with many rare water plants, with some here on the left protected from hungry ducks by cylinders of mesh.

Left
The Titan arum, the largest unbranched inflorescence on Earth, comes from the tropical rainforests of Indonesia. Long queues of people formed to see this rare flowering event in December 2015. Melbourne's gardening population turned up for the several days this remarkable flower was on show in the tropical hothouse at the Royal Botanic Gardens.

Above
An aerial view of the volcano as envisaged by Guilfoyle.

This cacti collection recently planted on the sloping banks of Guilfoyle's volcano is much admired by visitors. The original cactus garden nearby forms part of the original design, which is planted in such a way to represent lava flow spewing out of the volcano's centre.

A favourite pathway for many is through the Chinese Garden. It contains a remarkable variety of plants, including tree peonies, clumps of bamboo, ginger lilies and a fine *Ginkgo biloba* tree.

LA TROBE'S COTTAGE

Melbourne's early colonial Governor La Trobe was a very keen gardener. At his first Government House he decided to plant indigenous stock as well as exotics from his English home. The house was imported in portable demountable panels and assembled on site, first in Fitzroy Gardens and then on the King's Domain opposite the National Herbarium, where it has settled in well.

Sandi Pullman is the keen hands-on gardener responsible for keeping this historic garden as close as she can to its heritage guidelines.

Dianne Reilly, secretary of Melbourne's C. J. La Trobe Society, from research for her thesis on La Trobe, is equally keen to make sure his contribution to establishing Melbourne and this garden is accurately acknowledged.

Espaliered apple trees silhouette along the white weatherboard walls of the house

with herbaceous borders flowering for most of the year. La Trobe's cottage garden keeps to appropriate historic plantings, as well as including some native species that La Trobe himself admired.

Melbourne Grammar School

The plaque on this tree reads: 'Norfolk Island Pine Planted February 1st 1858. To celebrate Dr. J. E. Bromby's arrival at the school'. Bromby was Melbourne Grammar School's first headmaster. The tree, which is in good health now, was once in poor condition. In the 1950s the top 2 metres were in bad shape as the tree was being strangled by the bracket supporting a wireless aerial erected by boarders living nearby.

University of Melbourne

This tree, Cussonia spicata, was propagated from the original tree planted by Professor McCoy, one of the first four professors, in the 1880s. This unusual tree from Africa is the second tree to grace this courtyard, which is located near the university's Law School.

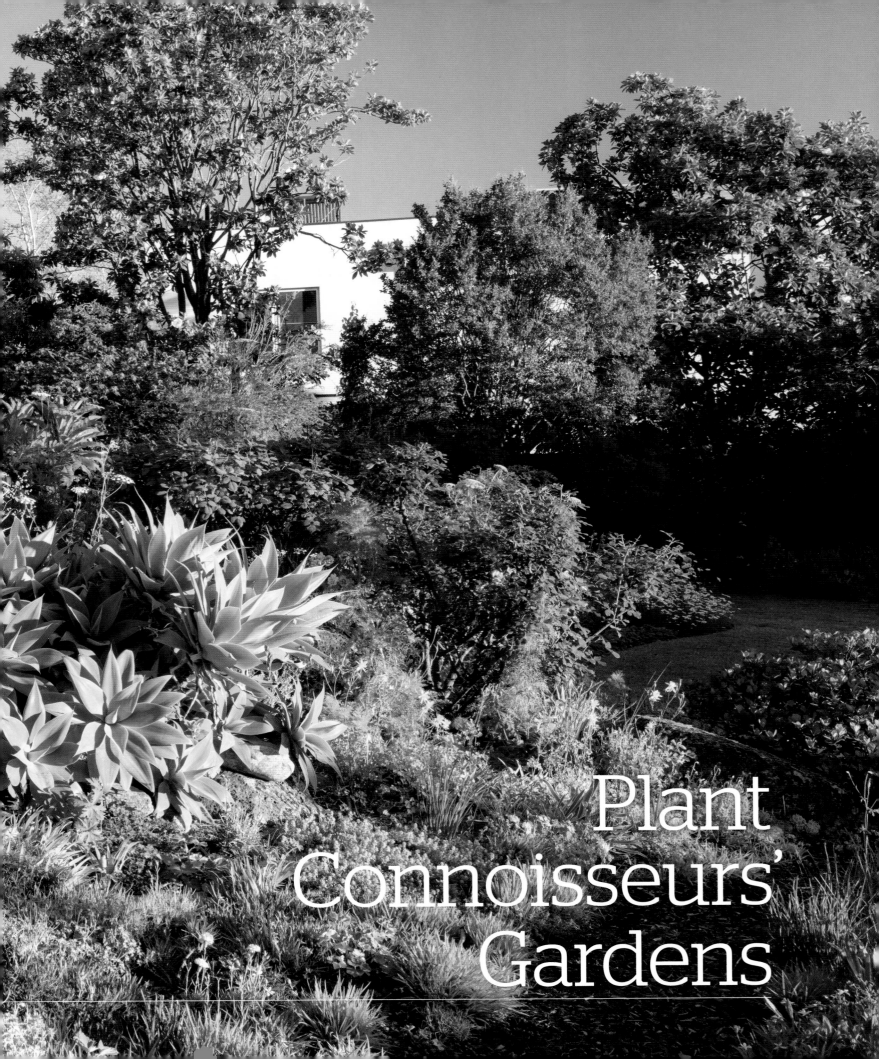

Plant
Connoisseurs'
Gardens

MAY ROAD

Caroline Davies and her late husband David Martin conducted popular garden tours, not only around noteworthy Melbourne gardens, but also nationally and internationally. Mediterranean gardens were their focus – including Corfu where Caroline's mother Daphne was born, and other Greek Islands – specialising in their native wildflowers. Caroline was amazed when she saw cyclamen growing wild in the mountains of Greece for the first time. She has her own collection of these tiny winter flowering plants potted in her courtyard.

Caroline believes that as a child her interest in gardening developed from her father, who was a keen gardener, as was his sister, who had a walled garden in Devon dating back to the Elizabethan period. Caroline and her younger brother David visited many Devon gardens as children with their parents, later moving with the family to Australia as teenagers.

The May Road courtyard garden is a potted horticultural treasure. Each plant seems to revel in healthy growth from its pot, some flowering all year round, in their south-facing yet sheltered conditions.

Caroline was elected president of the Mediterranean Garden Society, based in Athens in 2016.

Right
Melbourne's climate, which is similar to the Mediterranean, provides the perfect conditions for both exotic and native potted plants to thrive. These pots are moved around regularly by Caroline to maximise their visual impact from inside when in flower. Pictured here on the terrace is a Wollemi pine, tree begonias and tiny succulents.

Caroline has repurposed her rear car parking area to accomodate potted horticultural treasures. Below the balcony are sculptures, wall plaques, trees and flowering vireya rhododendron shrubs, all displaying contrasting effects of leaf texture against the terracotta tiled floor.

Right
Cheerful ox-eye daisies are low
growing so they are placed at the
front of this herbacious border.

ASHLEY GROVE

This is the third large garden created in Melbourne by owner Marian Brookes. In this garden the first priority was to cover the hard, straight lines with a softer boundary and provide shelter for the more tender plants. When this was achieved, then the more interesting work could begin.

'I have always been particularly interested in new plants and have experimented widely growing many varieties from imported seed, mainly from the UK', Marian says. 'Seed catalogues provide plenty of scope for inspiration. When new seeds arrive and are propagated, I am full of hope for what may come. Some grow, and some don't.

Over the past 30 years the garden's structure has taken shape around the interesting trees, shrubs and perennials that have done well and remained.'

Interesting and rare trees planted here include:

Bowkeria verticillata – Natal shell-flower from South Africa, cuttings recently given to Geelong Botanic Gardens, whose specimen had died.

Chionanthus retusus and *C. virginicus* – fringetrees from North America, which are rather unremarkable until they flower, and then are spectacular.

Prunus incisa 'Praecox' – from Japan, which provide relief from Melbourne's July chill, with their prolific white blossom.

Montanoa bipinnatifida and *M. leucantha* – daisy trees from Central America.

Euphorbia lambii – tree euphorbia from the Canary Islands.

Rothmannia globosa – a bell gardenia from South Africa.

The fine foliage of a simple group of sheoak trees on the back lawn contrasts with the densely planted border that include low alpine plants, perennials, agaves, roses, and Queen Anne's lace.

Left
The pale-green colour of agave and euphorbia complements flowering pink Japanese prunus.

Above
Fresh green hop vines climb up Marian's verandah posts. Her knowledge and skill in propagating from seeds means she has a vast range of rare plants in her garden.

VIEW STREET

The most amazing thing about this particular garden is that it is so close to city life but feels so enveloped by nature. Located mere minutes from Melbourne's city centre, Kate Herd and her family enjoy their exotic collection of plants, where natives thrive adjacent to exotic plantings around an attractive Victorian villa. Kate is a passionate gardener. She is also a garden designer and this is where she experiments with different plants and design techniques. View Street hosts local community activities that take place in the amphitheatre and there are tennis courts and walkways along the banks of the Yarra River.

Kate's extensive advice on growing vegetables in her book *Kitchen Gardens of Australia* is wonderfully demonstrated here in her large productive vegetable garden.

Down on the flood plain beside the Yarra, large river red gums grow along the banks.

Kate and her family have worked tirelessly over many years and managed to successfully keep introduced weeds at bay within this native bushland.

Right ·
Looking up towards the house
from the Yarra River bank,
native grasses and river red
gum trees are thriving after
years of weed clearing.

Narrow winding gravel paths
zigzag down from the house
through Kate's magical
shrubberies of exotic and native
plant material, including pink
pineapple lilies, white sea onions
and blue-grey cussonia.

An unusual acacia species that has fluffy white flowers that bloom on the main branch. These flowers remain in bloom for weeks, attracting bees and butterflies.

The broad gravel path follows the circumference of the round lawn, which serves as a performance amphitheatre with stepped terraces rising up the bank behind for audience seating.

AIREDALE AVENUE

ndrew Rouse is vice-president of the Australian Rhododendron Society of Victoria and has one of the most important vireya rhododendron collections in the world. The vast range of these exceptional flowering plants was started by his father Professor John Rouse when he was in Borneo and New Guinea during World War II on active service. Andrew has propagated many hybrids as well as maintaining a serious species collection.

Although Melbourne's climate allows vireyas to be planted outside, Andrew also uses two glasshouses situated along his back garden's fence to ensure the growth of an abundant collection.

Right
A bright crimson vireya
rhododendron flower is sprinkled
with Melbourne's spring
morning dew.

Vireya rhododendrons (including hybrids) come in every colour of the rainbow.

JOLIMONT TERRACE

Opposite the Melbourne Cricket Ground sits this charmingly small garden, which is lovingly attended to by Sarah Guest, the noteable garden writer. Thirty years ago, renowned Melbourne architect Guilford Bell offered to design lattice to 'cheer up' the north side passage of Sarah's large Victorian Terrace house, which was built in the 1860s. On this lattice, she has espaliered a camellia – *Camellia sasanqua* 'Mine No Yuki' (snow on the mountains) – now 30 years old. As stunningly supported topiary, it now spreads 5 metres long and 2 metres high and is the perfect example of formal flowering symmetry.

Sarah says: 'I enjoy playing with plants – tidy does not interest me – in fact to me the garden looks horribly neat in winter after its massive late autumn slashback, which is done for no better reason than the front door has been lost!

I love to mix formality with frilly, evergreen with deciduous, native with exotic – I am mad about bulbs, particularly if they are dormant in summer and do not need watering. Old coppers make brilliant plant containers and do not vie for attention with the plants they hold. I am addicted to plants and buy from our specialist plantsmen in and around Melbourne.

This tiny garden is almost entirely shaded. The soil is vile – grey sand which, after 30 years of expensive nourishment and wagons of elm leaves "stolen" from the park remains – grey sand!

'For the future – I do hope the espaliered camellias survive for the enjoyment of others – but I won't know, so I don't care!'

For over 30 years Sarah has carefully trained this sasanqua camellia to this amazingly long espaliered form on its timber support frame.

Below
The climbing rose 'Gold Bunny',
frames the side posts of this
gateway through which the
winning horses pass before
and after the Melbourne Cup
Carnival races.

FLEMINGTON RACECOURSE

Terry Freeman, Senior Manager of Flemington Grounds and Gardens for the Victoria Racing Club and his staff are proud people on Melbourne Cup Day. The world-famous race has been run in November each year since 1861. With the international sporting media attention focused on Melbourne, the roses are much photographed and need to be in full bloom. It seems that, regardless of weather vagaries, Terry's garden team achieves this with ease each year.

Terry says: 'There are 16,000 rose bushes at Flemington. On Derby Day, first day of Melbourne Cup Carnival, they look their best. The Melbourne Cup race is always the first Tuesday in November each year. My home garden, nearby, has a number of roses, most of which were planted as a trial to see if they would perform well at Flemington. The new French varieties are strong growers here.

'Byron Moore, secretary at Flemington for 44 years, once commented that he knew nothing about racing and knew more about roses. Had it been otherwise, Flemington would have been the poorer. One of Moore's great gardening friends was Alister Clark, Melbourne's famous rosarian. Clark bred many Australian rose varieties, often naming them after his many friends, such as Kitty Kininmoth and Lorraine Lee.

'We gardeners at Flemington are custodians of a great horticultural heritage asset.'

Vigorously flowering pink Grimaldi shrub roses are a welcome display in the car park. Massed together, they create an exhilarating scented show.

Thousands of racegoers move along broad paths under arches of Lamarque roses in flower. The sight and smell is both spectacular and memorable.

MARANOA GARDENS

In 1901, J. M. Watson purchased 1.4 hectares of land for a private garden, where he cultivated a collection of mainly Australian and New Zealand native species. After Watson's death in 1926, the council acquired the land and gradually removed all of the New Zealand natives, establishing Maranoa as one of the earliest Australian native botanical gardens. Four vegetation zones have been developed within the gardens: temperate woodland, arid rocky, dry forest and rainforest.

Maranoa Gardens is the only public native garden located in inner Melbourne and is home to over 4000 species of Australian natives spanning from all regions of Australia.

Cootamundra wattle (*Acacia baileyana*) flowers in mid-winter giving a warm golden glow to a chilly July Melbourne morning.

This gravel garden was developed in the 1980s as a well-drained display bed for Australian plants such as wattles, bottlebrushes and heaths.

Three Wollemi pines (*Wollemia nobilis*) discovered as recently as 1994 just north of Sydney, are planted closely together. These prehistoric trees reproduce both sexually (through wind pollination), and vegetatively, resulting in numerous trunks on each tree. Other native trees, including eucalypts and araucarias, are planted on this open lawn.

BIRRARUNG MARR

B irrarung Marr, on the Yarra River's north bank adjacent to Federation Square, is Melbourne's newest major park. It hosts many events and festivals. Near Princes Bridge, the park and gardens incorporate three terraces of contrasting grass and sand.

The lower terrace follows the curve of the Yarra River and retains sections of the original avenue of English elms (*Ulmus procera*). The middle terrace hosts temporary facilities linked to events held at the Melbourne Cricket Ground and other venues nearby. Great drifts of native and exotic plants, trees and shrubs are planted here. The upper terrace has views of the Arts Centre's spire and St Paul's Cathedral, as well as seasonal perennial displays on the slopes down to Batman Avenue.

The Birrarung Wilam installation celebrates the diversity of Victoria's Indigenous culture by interpreting stories through public artworks. A winding pathway acknowledges the significance of the eel as a traditional food source, and a semicircle of metal shields represents each of the five groups of the Kulin Nation.

Right
A simple, wild meadow mix of colourful wildflowers flourishes on this sloping bank at the end of Exhibition Street. The skyline of multi-storey buildings is behind, with an iconic Melbourne tram rolling past.

THE GARDENERS

Blair House Maggie Nanut

Coonac Jane Hansen and James Stewart

Cranlana Anna Thompson, Clifford Aarons, Pasco Thompson and Anne Nadenbousch

D'Estaville Bronwyn Cathels

Eulinya Shane Hester and Paula Fox

Raheen Jessica Hempel and Sadie Jenkyn

Government House Kate Bower

Grandview Grove Lewis Bell

Clendon Court Fiona Myer

Marne Street Helen Blythe and Paul Bangay

Kensington Road Philippa Springall

Tivoli Road Peter Lovell

Melbourne Club John Fordham

Caroline House Patrice O'Brien and Deni

Topiary Garden Su Dihn

Tintern Vanessa Kennedy and Penny Dunn

Glenbervie Road Donna Somerville and Samantha Baillieu

Avoca Street Sally-Ann Hains

Grant Avenue Donna Sommerville

Rippon Lea Justin Buckley

Struan Street The late Susan Renouf

Domain Road David Wilkinson

Douglas Street Jenny Lempriere

Yar-Orrong Road Libby Morgan

Kooyong Road Robert Boyle and Mandy Mandie

Camellia Balcony Betty Spangaro

Vermont South Pamela Jefferson

Spring Street Primrose Potter

Northcote Courtyard Bill Henson

Richmond House Antoinette Nido, Angelina Nido and Peter Mulqueeny

Bishopscourt Philip Freier

Old Colonists' Gardens Judith Ormandy

Royal Botanic Gardens Andrew Laidlaw, Terry Smyth and Matthew Howard.

Royal Botanic Gardens Tim Entwistle

La Trobe's Cottage Sandi Pullman

May Road Caroline Davies

Ashley Grove Marion Brookes and Ginger

View Street Kate Herd and Inka

Airedale Avenue Andrew Rouse and Bobby

Jolimont Terrace Sarah Guest

Flemington Racecourse Terry Freeman

Maranoa Gardens David Birch

DEDICATION

For Bibi, Edward, Oliver, Artemis and Angus.
DW

And for Deborah, Raffaella, Romy and Isabella.
KB

First published in Australia in 2017
This edition reprinted in 2018
by Thames & Hudson Australia Pty Ltd
11 Central Boulevard Portside Business Park
Port Melbourne Victoria 3207

ABN: 72 004 751 964

www.thameshudson.com.au

© David Wilkinson (text) 2017
© Kimbal Baker (photography) 2017

20 19 18   5 4 3 2

The moral right of the author has been asserted.

ISBN: 9780500501146

National Library of Australia
Cataloguing-in-Publication entry

Grand Melbourne Gardens/written by David Wilkinson;
photography by Kimbal Baker
9780500501146 (hardback)

Gardens—Victoria—Melbourne—Pictorial works.
Historic gardens—Victoria—Melbourne—Pictorial works.
Photography of gardens—Victoria—Melbourne.
Wilkinson, David, author. Baker, Kimbal, photographer.

Design: Fiona James
Editing: Neil Conning
Photograph of Kate Herd on page 211
by Ponch Hawkes
Printed and bound in China by Imago

ACKNOWLEDGEMENTS

To the gardeners, who supported this book
so wholeheartedly, we thank you. Thanks also
to Mike Petty, Neil Conning, Fiona James and
Andrew Holford. Sincere thanks also to C R Kennedy
for the magnificent Pentax 645s series camera
and Robert Kennedy for piloting the DJI Inspire
1 pro drone with the DJI Zenmuse x5 camera
for the photograph on pages 4-5 and 167.